Introduction:

## A. How Music Changed:

Music has undergone a significant transformation in recent years. Gone are the days of CDs and cassette tapes ruling the industry and vinyl has long been reduced to little more than a thing of nostalgia.  Instead, we're now in the era of digital streaming, where platforms like Spotify, Apple Music, and YouTube dominate how we consume music. This shift has revolutionized not only how music is distributed but also how artists are discovered, promoted, and managed.

## B. Streaming's Impact:

The rise of streaming services has had a profound impact on the music industry, reshaping the way artists connect with their audiences and earn a living. With streaming, listeners have instant access to millions of songs at their fingertips, changing the dynamics of music consumption. This has brought both opportunities and challenges for recording artists and their managers. Understanding this new landscape is crucial for effectively navigating the digital stage.

The impact of streaming on the music industry is exemplified by the top three international streaming artists, whose success highlights the significant revenue generated from streamed

content:

• Taylor Swift: With over 26.1 billion global streams in 2023 alone, Taylor Swift was the Worlds most streamed artist. Her catalog of music has amassed substantial gross receipts from streamed content, contributing to her overall success as an artist in the streaming era. In fact Taylor earned over $170 million in royalties from Spotify streaming services.

• Drake: As another top streaming artist, Drake closed out 2023 as the most streamed rapper on Spotify with 17.6 Billion streams. His immense popularity on streaming platforms has translated into almost 300 million in Spotify earnings giving him the top spot in total earnings from streamed content, showcasing the financial rewards available to artists who effectively leverage the streaming landscape.

• Ed Sheeran: Known for his chart-topping hits and massive streaming numbers,  is among the top international streaming artists. His extensive catalog of music has amassed over 46 billion streams, resulting in over 185 million from streamed content and demonstrating the lucrative opportunities available to artists in the streaming era.

C. What This Book Covers:

In this book, we'll explore the ins and outs of managing recording artists in today's streaming marketplace. From understanding the streaming landscape and maximizing revenue to building a strong digital brand and engaging with fans online, we'll cover essential strategies and best practices for success. Whether you're an aspiring artist manager, an industry professional, or an artist looking to take control of your career, this book will provide valuable insights and practical advice to help you thrive in the digital age of music.

II. Understanding The Streaming Landscape:

A. Overview of Major Streaming Platforms:

The streaming landscape is diverse, with several major platforms vying for listeners' attention. Platforms like Spotify, Apple Music, Amazon Music, and YouTube Music offer different features and user experiences. Understanding the strengths and weaknesses of each platform is essential for artists and their managers to make informed decisions about where to distribute their music and focus their promotional efforts.

B. Key Metrics and Analytics for Artist Success:

In the digital age, data is king. Streaming platforms provide artists and their teams with access to a wealth of analytics and metrics that can offer valuable insights into their audience demographics, listening habits, and geographic reach. Understanding key metrics such as streams, followers, playlist placements, and listener engagement is crucial for evaluating an artist's success and informing strategic decisions about marketing, touring, and content creation.

C. Trends and Challenges in the Streaming Marketplace:

The streaming marketplace is constantly evolving, with new trends and challenges emerging regularly. From the rise of playlist culture and algorithmic discovery to the impact of social media influencers and the challenge of standing out in a crowded digital landscape, artists and their managers must stay abreast of the latest trends and adapt their strategies accordingly. Additionally, challenges such as fair compensation for artists, combating streaming fraud, and navigating complex licensing agreements require careful attention and proactive management strategies.

D. Pay Per Stream Data Points:

In addition to understanding the various streaming platforms available, it's essential for artists and their management teams to be aware of the pay per stream data associated with each platform. This data provides insights into how much artists can expect to earn for each stream of their music. While the exact payout per stream varies depending on factors such as the artist's contract terms, country of streaming, and the streaming platform itself, here's a general overview:

• Spotify: On average, artists can expect to earn between $0.003 and $0.005 per stream on Spotify. However, this amount can fluctuate based on factors such as the listener's subscription status (free vs. premium) and the artist's share of streams within their respective genre.

• Apple Music: Apple Music typically offers slightly higher payouts per stream compared to Spotify, with artists earning around $0.006 to $0.007 per stream. Like Spotify, the exact payout can vary based on factors such as listener demographics and subscription status.

• Amazon Music: Amazon Music pays artists approximately $0.004 to $0.008 per stream, depending on factors such as the artist's distribution agreement and the listener's subscription status.

• YouTube Music: YouTube Music's payout structure is more complex, as it involves revenue generated from both ad-supported streams and YouTube Premium subscriptions. On average, artists can expect to earn around $0.001 to $0.003 per stream on YouTube Music.

Understanding these pay per stream data points is crucial

for artists and their management teams to make informed decisions about their distribution strategies, promotional efforts, and revenue projections across various streaming platforms.

III. Building and Maintaining Online Presence:

A. Social Media Strategies for Artists:

Social media has become a powerful tool for artists to connect with their fans, build their brand, and promote their music. Artists and their management teams must develop effective social media strategies that align with their brand identity and target audience. This includes choosing the right platforms to focus on (e.g., Instagram, Twitter, TikTok), creating engaging content that resonates with fans, and maintaining a consistent posting schedule to keep followers engaged.

One platform in particular is emerging as a must use asset in growing a fanbase as a music content creator, that platform is called Tin-Tok.

Utilizing TikTok to Grow Your Fanbase as a Music Artist:

TikTok has emerged as a powerful platform for music artists to connect with fans, showcase their talent, and grow their fanbase. Here are some key strategies for leveraging TikTok effectively:

Create Engaging Content:

TikTok thrives on short, entertaining content, create videos that are visually appealing, engaging, and showcase your music in a unique way. This could include sharing snippets of your songs, behind-the-scenes footage of your creative process, or even participating in popular TikTok challenges and trends.

Utilize Music-Driven Challenges and Trends:

TikTok is known for its viral challenges and trends, many of which are centered around music. Keep an eye on trending hashtags and challenges related to music, and participate in them by creating your own unique twist that showcases your music and personality. This can help expose your music to a wider audience and attract new fans.

Collaborate with Influencers and Creators:

Collaborating with TikTok influencers and creators can help amplify your reach and introduce your music to their followers. Identify influencers or creators whose content aligns with your music and reach out to them for potential collaborations, such as using your music in their videos or creating promotional content together.

Engage with Your Audience:

TikTok is all about building community and engagement, so be sure to interact with your audience by responding to comments, engaging with duets and stitch videos featuring your music, and participating in live streams. Building genuine connections with your fans can help foster loyalty and encourage them to support your music.

Optimize Your Profile and Use Hashtags:

Make sure your TikTok profile is optimized to showcase your music and brand effectively. Use a catchy profile picture, write a compelling bio that highlights your music and personality, and include links to your music and social media profiles. Additionally, use relevant hashtags in your videos to increase discoverability and reach on the platform.

Promote Your Music:

Don't be afraid to directly promote your music on

TikTok. Share previews of your latest releases, encourage users to check out your music on streaming platforms, and even run TikTok ads to reach a targeted audience. Just be sure to balance promotional content with engaging and entertaining content to keep your audience interested.

By implementing these strategies and consistently sharing engaging content, music artists can effectively utilize TikTok to grow their fanbase, increase their reach, and promote their music to a wider audience.

B. Creating Engaging Content for Digital Platforms:

In the digital age, content is king. Artists must continuously create compelling content to keep their audience engaged and attract new listeners. This includes not only music releases but also behind-the-scenes footage, live performances, music videos, and interactive experiences. By leveraging a variety of content types and platforms (e.g., Tik-Tok, YouTube, Instagram Stories, Facebook Live), artists can maintain a strong online presence and foster deeper connections with their fans.

C. Leveraging Digital Marketing Tools and Techniques:

Digital marketing plays a crucial role in promoting artists and their music in today's online landscape. Artists and their management teams should leverage a range of digital marketing tools and techniques to reach and engage their target audience. This includes email marketing campaigns, social media advertising, influencer partnerships, search engine optimization (SEO), and data-driven targeting strategies. By implementing effective digital marketing strategies, artists can expand their reach, increase their fan base, and drive streams and sales of their music.

Building marketing funnels to drive potential fans to your music involves a strategic approach to attract, engage, and convert listeners into fans. Here's a step-by-step guide on how to build effective marketing funnels:

Define Your Target Audience:

Identify your ideal listener demographic based on factors like age, gender, location, and music preferences. Understanding your target audience will help tailor your marketing messages and strategies to resonate with them effectively.

Create Compelling Content:

Produce high-quality music and content that showcases

your unique style and resonates with your target audience. This includes releasing singles, music videos, behind-the-scenes footage, live performances, and engaging social media content.

Attract Attention:

Use various marketing channels to attract potential fans to your music. This can include social media advertising, influencer partnerships, email marketing, content marketing, and search engine optimization (SEO) techniques.

Engage and Capture:

Once you've attracted attention, engage with your audience and capture their interest. Encourage listeners to follow you on social media, subscribe to your email list, or join your fan community. Offer incentives such as exclusive content, discounts on merchandise, or access to pre-releases to incentivize engagement.

Nurture Relationships:

Build and nurture relationships with your audience by

consistently providing value and engaging with them on a personal level. Respond to comments and messages, share behind-the-scenes glimpses into your life and music-making process, and show appreciation for your fans' support.

Convert to Fans:

Convert engaged listeners into fans by offering them opportunities to support you further. This can include promoting your music on streaming platforms, purchasing merchandise, attending live events or virtual concerts, or joining your fan club or Patreon community.

Measure and Optimize:

Continuously monitor and measure the performance of your marketing funnels using analytics tools. Track key metrics such as website traffic, social media engagement, email open rates, and conversion rates to identify areas for improvement and optimize your marketing strategies accordingly.

By following these steps and consistently refining your

marketing funnels, you can effectively drive potential fans to your music and grow your fanbase over time.

IV. Crafting a Digital Brand Identity:

A. Establishing an Authentic Brand Narrative:

In the digital age, a strong brand narrative is essential for artists to differentiate themselves and connect with their audience on a deeper level. This involves defining the artist's unique story, values, and personality, and communicating it consistently across all digital channels. By crafting an authentic brand narrative, artists can create a compelling and memorable identity that resonates with fans and helps them stand out in a crowded marketplace.

B. Visual Branding:

Artwork, Imagery, and Merchandise:

Visual branding plays a crucial role in shaping an artist's digital brand identity. This includes artwork for music releases, promotional images, logos, and branding elements that reflect the artist's style and personality. Additionally, artists can leverage merchandise such as apparel, accessories, and collectibles to further reinforce their brand identity and provide fans with tangible ways to connect with their music and persona.

As a recording artist, you can leverage AI-powered design

tools and platforms to create promotional graphics for flyers, cover art, social media posts, new merchandise, etc. Here's how you can do it:

AI-Powered Design Tools:

Utilize AI-powered design tools such as Canva, Adobe Spark, or Designhill. These platforms offer user-friendly interfaces and templates that artists can customize to create professional-looking graphics for various promotional purposes.

Automated Design Generation:

Some AI-driven design platforms offer automated design generation features that use machine learning algorithms to analyze your brand and preferences, then generate design options tailored to your style. Platforms like Bing image creator, Midjourney, Starryai, and many others  can save valuable time and effort in the design process while ensuring consistency across your promotional materials.

Customizable Templates:

Look for AI design tools that offer customizable

templates specifically designed for musicians and recording artists. These templates may include pre-designed layouts for album covers, social media posts, merchandise designs, and more, allowing you to easily create cohesive branding across different platforms.

Image Recognition and Editing:

AI-powered design platforms often come equipped with advanced image recognition and editing capabilities. This allows you to easily edit photos, manipulate images, and create visually striking graphics for your promotional materials.

Personalization and A/B Testing:

Take advantage of AI-driven personalization features to tailor your promotional graphics to specific audience segments or demographics. Additionally, some platforms offer A/B testing capabilities that enable you to experiment with different design variations and determine which ones resonate best with your audience.

Integration with Social Media Platforms:

Look for AI design tools that integrate seamlessly with popular social media platforms like Instagram, Facebook, and Twitter. This allows you to create and schedule promotional posts directly from the design platform, streamlining your social media marketing efforts.

By leveraging AI-powered design tools and platforms, recording artists can create visually compelling and engaging promotional graphics for flyers, cover art, social media posts, and merchandise, helping to attract new fans and grow their audience online.

C. Consistency Across Digital Platforms:

Consistency is key to building a strong digital brand identity. Artists must ensure that their brand messaging, visual elements, and tone of voice remain consistent across all digital platforms, including social media, streaming profiles, websites, and email newsletters. This consistency helps reinforce the artist's identity and build brand recognition among fans, making it easier for them to connect with and engage with the artist's content.

V. Maximizing Streaming Revenue:

A. Monetization Strategies for Recording Artists:

In the streaming era, recording artists have multiple avenues for monetizing their music beyond traditional album sales. This includes revenue streams such as streaming royalties, digital downloads, merchandise sales, concert ticket sales, and licensing opportunities. Artists and their management teams must explore and implement a variety of monetization strategies to maximize their earnings and sustain their music careers in the digital age.

B. Understanding Royalties and Streaming Payouts:

It's crucial for artists to understand how streaming royalties are calculated and distributed to ensure they're maximizing their earnings from streaming platforms. This involves understanding the various types of royalties (e.g., mechanical royalties, performance royalties, sync royalties), as well as how streaming platforms calculate payouts based on factors like streaming volume, subscriber revenue, and territory-specific rates. By understanding the nuances of streaming royalties, artists can make informed decisions about their distribution strategies and negotiate fair deals with streaming platforms.

The Harry Fox Agency (HFA) is a provider of rights management and collector and distributor of mechanical license fees on behalf of music publishers in the United States. HFA has over 48,000 music publishing clients and issues the largest number of licenses for physical and digital formats of music.Registering your music with a Performing Rights Organization (PRO) or Collective Management Organization (CMO) is an important step to ensure that you receive royalties for the public performance of your music. Here's how to register your music with a PRO or CMO:

Research PROs or CMOs:

• Start by researching different PROs or CMOs in your country or region. Some of the well-known PROs include ASCAP, BMI, SESAC (in the United States), PRS for Music (in the UK), SOCAN (in Canada), and many others.

• Learn about the services they offer, their membership requirements, fee structures, and how they distribute royalties to their members.

Choose the Right PRO or CMO:

• Consider factors such as the genre of your music, your target audience, and the PRO or CMO's reputation and reach when choosing the right organization for you.

• Each PRO or CMO may have different membership

criteria, so make sure you meet their eligibility requirements before applying for membership.

Join the PRO or CMO:

• Once you've chosen a PRO or CMO, you'll need to apply for membership. This typically involves filling out an application form, providing information about yourself and your music, and paying any applicable membership fees.

• Some PROs or CMOs may require you to submit proof of ownership of your music, such as copyright registrations or ISRC codes.

Register Your Music:

• After becoming a member of the PRO or CMO, you'll need to register your music with them. This involves providing details about each of your songs, including the title, composer(s), publisher(s), and any other relevant information.

• Depending on the PRO or CMO, you may be able to register your music online through their member portal or by submitting physical registration forms.

Monitor and Manage Your Catalog:


• Keep track of your registered songs and catalog with the PRO or CMO. Make sure to update your information if there are any changes to your songs or ownership details.

• Monitor your royalty statements and payments from the PRO or CMO to ensure that you are receiving proper compensation for the public performance of your music.


Stay Informed:


• Stay informed about the services and resources offered by your chosen PRO or CMO. Many organizations offer educational workshops, networking events, and other resources to help their members succeed in the music industry.


By following these steps and registering your music with a PRO or CMO, you can ensure that you are properly represented and compensated for the public performance of your music.

On the digital side of the house be sure to register with SoundExchange and Songtrust to collect domestic and international royalties online:

SoundExchange:

- SoundExchange is a nonprofit organization that collects and distributes digital performance royalties on behalf of recording artists and record labels.

- It primarily deals with digital performance royalties, which are royalties paid by digital music services (such as Pandora, Spotify, Apple Music, etc.) for the streaming of sound recordings.

- SoundExchange collects these royalties from digital music services and distributes them to the rights holders, including recording artists, featured performers, background musicians, and record labels.

- Artists and rights holders need to register with SoundExchange to ensure they receive their royalties for digital performances of their music.


Songtrust:


- Songtrust is a music rights management platform that helps songwriters, composers, and music publishers collect royalties from various sources, including mechanical royalties, performance royalties, synchronization royalties, and more.

- Songtrust acts as a publishing administrator,

collecting royalties on behalf of songwriters and publishers worldwide.

- It offers services such as global royalty collection, registration of songs with collection societies, monitoring of royalty statements, and administration of licensing and synchronization deals.

- Songwriters and publishers can sign up with Songtrust to manage and maximize their royalty collection from various revenue streams, including digital streaming, radio airplay, TV placements, and more.

In summary, SoundExchange focuses on collecting and distributing digital performance royalties for sound recordings, while Songtrust collects performance and mechanical royalties from about 98% of the global music publishing market. If you use Songtrust, you have access to 65 societies and 215 countries/territories, reducing the need to register your works in multiple places.. Both organizations play important roles in ensuring that artists and rights holders receive proper compensation for the use of their music.

C. Negotiating Deals with Streaming Platforms:

As streaming continues to dominate the music industry,

artists and their management teams must navigate the landscape of negotiating deals with streaming platforms to ensure they're getting fair compensation for their music. This involves understanding the terms and conditions of streaming agreements, negotiating favorable royalty rates and revenue splits, and exploring additional opportunities for promotional support and marketing initiatives. By effectively negotiating deals with streaming platforms, artists can maximize their streaming revenue and build sustainable careers in the digital music marketplace.

VI. Engaging with Fans in the Digital Space:

A. Building a Strong Fan Community Online:

Engaging with fans in the digital space begins with building a strong online community centered around the artist's music and brand. This involves creating dedicated fan groups on social media platforms, establishing fan forums or communities on the artist's website, and encouraging fan-generated content such as fan art, covers, and remixes. By fostering a sense of belonging and community among fans, artists can cultivate a loyal and dedicated fan base that actively supports and promotes their music.

B. Utilizing Fan Engagement Tools and Platforms:

In addition to traditional social media platforms, artists

can leverage specialized fan engagement tools and platforms to connect with their audience in meaningful ways. This includes fan engagement platforms like Patreon, where fans can support artists through subscriptions and exclusive content, as well as fan engagement apps and platforms that offer interactive experiences such as virtual meet-and-greets, live Q&A sessions, and exclusive behind-the-scenes content. By utilizing these tools and platforms, artists can deepen their relationship with fans and offer unique experiences that drive engagement and loyalty.

C. Creating Memorable Digital Fan Experiences:

Engaging with fans in the digital space is about more than just posting content on social media; it's about creating memorable and meaningful experiences that resonate with fans on a personal level. This could include organizing virtual concerts or live-streamed performances on platforms like, Maestro, Panopto, Movie or livestream. Also, hosting online listening parties or album release events or launching interactive fan challenges and contests on sites like Bandcamp or Zoom can pay long term dividends as well. By creating immersive and interactive digital experiences, artists can forge deeper connections with their fans and create moments that leave a lasting impression.

VII. Collaborating in the Digital Age:

A. Collaborating with Other Artists and Producers Online:

The digital age has made it easier than ever for artists to collaborate with other musicians, producers, and creatives from around the world. Artists can connect with collaborators online through platforms like SoundCloud, Splice, and BandLab, allowing them to work together remotely and exchange ideas seamlessly. By leveraging digital collaboration tools and platforms, artists can expand their creative network and collaborate with a diverse range of talent, regardless of geographical boundaries.

B. Managing Virtual Collaborations and Remote Sessions:

Collaborating in the digital age requires effective management of virtual collaborations and remote recording sessions. This involves coordinating schedules across different time zones, establishing clear communication channels, and utilizing digital collaboration tools such as project management software, cloud-based storage platforms, and real-time messaging apps. By implementing efficient workflows and communication protocols, artists can streamline the collaboration process and ensure that projects stay on track, even when working with remote collaborators.

C. Leveraging Collaborative Platforms and Tools:

Artists can leverage a variety of collaborative platforms and tools to facilitate online collaborations and enhance the creative process. This includes platforms like Splice and Blend, which enable artists to share project files and collaborate on music production in real-time, as well as virtual collaboration tools like Zoom and Skype for remote meetings and brainstorming sessions. Additionally, cloud-based storage platforms like Dropbox and Google Drive provide secure and accessible storage solutions for sharing files and assets with collaborators. By leveraging these collaborative platforms and tools, artists can foster a collaborative and creative environment that encourages innovation and experimentation.

VIII. Protecting Intellectual Property Online:

A. Understanding Copyright Laws in the Digital Space:

In the digital age, it's crucial for artists and creators to have a solid understanding of copyright laws and how they apply to their work online. This includes understanding the rights granted by copyright law, such as the exclusive rights to reproduce, distribute, and publicly perform their work, as well as the limitations and exceptions to these rights. Additionally, artists should be aware of the Digital Millennium Copyright Act (DMCA) and its provisions for addressing copyright infringement online.

B. Strategies for Protecting Music and Artwork Online:

Protecting intellectual property online requires

implementing strategies to safeguard music, artwork, and other creative works from unauthorized use and exploitation. This includes registering copyrights for original works, using digital rights management (DRM) tools to control access to digital files, and watermarking or embedding metadata in digital assets to deter unauthorized distribution. Artists should also monitor online platforms and social media channels for instances of copyright infringement and take prompt action to address unauthorized use of their work.

C. Dealing with Copyright Infringement and Piracy:

Despite best efforts to protect intellectual property online, artists may still encounter instances of copyright infringement and piracy. When faced with copyright infringement, artists have several options for recourse, including sending cease-and-desist notices, filing DMCA takedown requests with online platforms, and pursuing legal action against infringers. Additionally, artists can take proactive measures to combat piracy by offering their work through legitimate channels, educating fans about the importance of supporting artists through legal means, and collaborating with industry stakeholders to develop effective anti-piracy initiatives. By taking a proactive approach to protecting intellectual property online, artists can safeguard their creative works and preserve their rights in the digital space.

IX. Navigating Digital Distribution Channels:

A. Working with Digital Distributors and Aggregators:

Digital distribution has become the primary method for artists to share their music with audiences worldwide. Artists can choose to work with digital distributors and aggregators, such as TuneCore, CD Baby, United Artists and DistroKid, to distribute their music to online platforms like Spotify, Apple Music, and Amazon Music. These services handle the technical aspects of distribution, including encoding, metadata management, and delivery to streaming platforms, allowing artists to focus on creating music while reaching a global audience.

B. Choosing the Right Distribution Strategy for Each Release:

Artists must carefully consider their distribution strategy for each release to maximize reach and revenue. This includes deciding whether to release music exclusively on certain platforms or make it available across multiple platforms simultaneously. Artists may also choose to release singles, EPs, or full-length albums and tailor their distribution strategy accordingly. Additionally, artists should consider factors such as release timing, marketing plans, and fan engagement strategies when planning their distribution approach.

C. Managing Release Strategies in the Streaming Era:

The streaming era has transformed how artists release and promote their music. Artists must develop comprehensive release strategies that leverage the power of streaming platforms to maximize exposure and engagement. This includes planning pre-release marketing campaigns to build anticipation, securing placements on curated playlists to reach new listeners, and engaging with fans through social media and other digital channels to drive streams and engagement. By strategically managing their release strategies in the streaming era, artists can optimize their chances of success in the digital distribution landscape.

X. Adapting to Emerging Technologies:

A. Embracing AI and Machine Learning in Artist Management:

The emergence of artificial intelligence (AI) and machine learning technologies is revolutionizing the way artist management operates. AI-powered analytics tools can provide insights into audience behavior, helping managers make data-driven decisions about marketing strategies, tour planning, and content creation. Machine learning algorithms can also assist in predicting trends and identifying opportunities for artists to capitalize on emerging markets or genres. Embracing AI and machine learning allows artist managers to stay ahead of the curve and optimize their strategies for success in the digital age.

One of the most useful advances in AI streaming technology is the development and refinement of personalized recommendation algorithms. Streaming platforms have been increasingly utilizing advanced AI algorithms to analyze user preferences, behaviors, and listening habits to provide personalized recommendations for music, podcasts, and other content. These recommendation systems leverage machine learning techniques to continuously improve the accuracy and relevance of recommendations, enhancing the user experience and increasing engagement on streaming platforms. Additionally, AI-driven content curation tools have emerged to assist artists, labels, and curators in creating personalized playlists and content collections tailored to specific listener demographics and preferences. These innovations in AI streaming technology aim to enhance content discovery, increase user engagement, and ultimately drive growth and retention for streaming platforms and content creators.

B. Exploring Virtual Reality and Augmented Reality

Experiences:

Virtual reality (VR) and augmented reality (AR) technologies offer new avenues for artists to engage with their fans and create immersive experiences. Artists can explore VR and AR platforms to host virtual concerts, create interactive music videos, and offer fans unique experiences such as virtual meet-and-greets or behind-the-scenes tours. These technologies enable artists to connect with fans in innovative ways, breaking down geographical barriers and offering a new level of intimacy and immersion in the digital space.

C. Staying Ahead of Technological Advancements in the Industry:

In the rapidly evolving landscape of the music industry, it's essential for artist managers to stay abreast of the latest technological advancements and trends. This involves keeping a pulse on emerging technologies such as blockchain, NFTs (non-fungible tokens), and decentralized platforms, which have the potential to disrupt traditional models of music distribution, rights management, and fan engagement. By staying ahead of technological advancements, artist managers can identify new opportunities for their clients, adapt their strategies to changing consumer behaviors, and remain competitive in the digital marketplace.

XI. Conclusion:

A. Recap of Key Points:

Throughout this book, we've explored the intricacies of managing recording artists in the digital age, focusing on strategies to navigate the streaming marketplace, build a strong online presence, and protect intellectual property. We've discussed the importance of understanding streaming platforms, maximizing revenue streams, engaging with fans online, collaborating in the digital space, and adapting to emerging technologies.

B. Future Outlook for Digital Artist Management:

As technology continues to evolve and reshape the music industry, the future of digital artist management holds both opportunities and challenges. Advancements in AI, VR, AR, and other emerging technologies will continue to revolutionize how artists connect with their audience and monetize their music. However, artists and their management teams must also navigate evolving consumer behaviors, streaming algorithms, and copyright laws to remain competitive in the ever-changing digital landscape.

C. Final Thoughts and Recommendations:

In closing, effective artist management in the digital age

requires a combination of creativity, adaptability, and strategic thinking. By embracing digital tools and platforms, staying informed about industry trends, and prioritizing fan engagement and creativity, artists and their management teams can thrive in the streaming marketplace and build sustainable careers in the digital music landscape. As the industry continues to evolve, it's essential for artists and their managers to remain agile, innovative, and proactive in navigating the challenges and opportunities of the digital era.